Into a teenage heart....What keeps me awake at night

Aashi Singh

BookLeaf Publishing

Presentation by *BookLeaf Publishing*

Web: www.bookleafpub.com

E-mail: info@bookleafpub.com

ISBN: 9789358731767

First edition 2024

DEDICATION

To my parents,

who gifted me my first book about 10 years ago

and encouraged me to constantly read, write
and explore

ACKNOWLEDGEMENT

I would like to express my sincere thanks to the following people and institutions that made this book possible.

To BookLeaf Publishing for creating an opportunity and enabling me with all possible help to publish this book.

To my father who inspired, challenged, reviewed and pushed me for making the effort come to fruition. He motivated me by showing me his own handwritten collection of poems that he wrote in his teens but never published. Dad, now that this one is published - it's time we get yours published too.

To my mom, who is such an inspiration for me - I have seen her patiently managing home, her startup, her studies, her mom, her sessions where she is a mentor to young girls setting up social businesses and yet finds time to read, to write, to cook my favourite meals for me. Mom, you are the best!

To my teachers at my previous school AuroMirra International, Bangalore and my current school, GEMS Modern Academy, Dubai who have always been inspiring me towards my creative expression.

And finally, to all those special friends who, knowingly and unknowingly, are the muse for these 21 poems.

FOREWORD

What keeps teenagers awake at night?

It is with a sense of pride and admiration that I introduce you to a young lady who with her poetic prowess and depth of emotion has effortlessly brought together a collection of verses that will resonate with every teenager: Aashi.

This oft-explored narrative comes from a youngster who is experiencing it firsthand and reflecting as she goes through life with all its trials and tribulations. I smiled as I read this line in *A Red hot flame* - 'How very much I had been in my head…' that seems to be the story of every teenager's life!

As her principal, in Aashi, I have witnessed a maturity way beyond her years. Her compassionate nature sets her apart and she has a heart that worries deeply about the befuddling occurrences she is witnessing and tries to make sense of it. She seeks understanding using the lens of sensitivity and interpretation, limited by her experiences but expanded by her imagination. Sometimes you must read her poems twice over, as the nuances make you pause and compel you to reflect. Her poems are an expression of the emotions that dwell within her own soul.

If Aashi's caring and empathic nature makes her appear to be vulnerable, she is working to be a physically strong lass as she yearns to master the ancient art of Kalarippayattu. These poems are a window into a teenage heart – fragile yet resilient, troubled yet optimistic, edgy yet filled with imaginings. Aashi's thoughts serve as a poignant reminder to educators, parents and teenagers that within each young heart lie thoughts that need to be understood, supported and nurtured.

I wish her all the best as she embarks on her inner journey. She will go on to make a positive difference - of that I have no doubt.

Best wishes,

Nargish Khambatta
Principal
Senior Vice President, Education

PREFACE

This book is a collection of 21 poems written by a teenager pouring her heart and soul into each and every one of them. These poems explore a range of emotions and experiences that are common to many young people growing up today, such as love, heartbreak, self-discovery, and finding one's place in the world.

Through the poems, you are invited into the world of a teenage heart and you would be given a tour of what it's like to navigate the complexities of adolescence in the 21st century. As you read these poems, you may find yourself nodding in recognition, or perhaps even experiencing a sense of empathy or connection with me. It is my hope that this book will not only entertain and inspire you, but also offer a window into the mind and heart of a young person, on the brink of adulthood. Remember, there could be someone close to you, feeling exactly the same.

So, without further ado, I invite you to delve into this collection of poems and experience the beauty and power of youth in all its raw and unfiltered glory.

Under the Streetlamp

I stood and watched
As a streetlamp slowly flickered
Beginning to die away

Under that very streetlamp
A pair of bright green eyes I saw
Or rather it saw me
Baffled, my new feline friend knew I was there
Although, it glared as if it were looking through
me.

Moments later,
As if I were there no more
The cat ran away

A man, in a coat I saw running on the street
across
Noticing me asked
What a girl like myself would be doing out
So very late
Baffled, I asked whatever is it I'm wearing
Accurate his answer
Confused his tone

I noticed, in a hurry he was
I bid him farewell
The man ran away

All day, till now
I've sat on this bench
Under the streetlamp
Not a bird on a tree
Not a man on the streets
Noticed me
I thought to myself
Surely… I still am a ghost? A formless spirit?

I sat and watched
As the streetlamp slowly flickered
And finally died away.

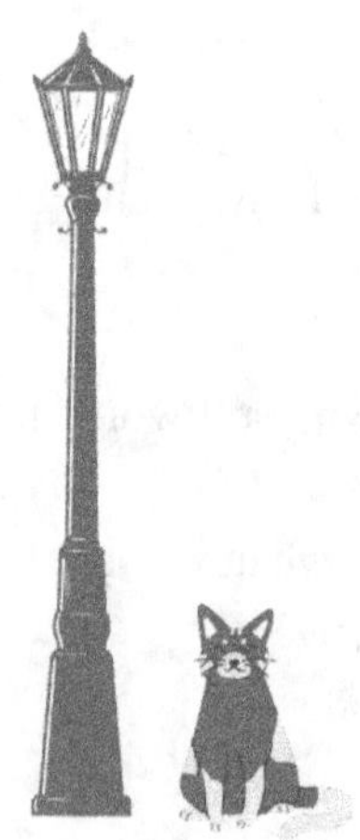

When the clock strikes none

She should be asleep
But she's not
But they could never know
What she really does
When the clock strikes none

She felt numb
As if her tears can no longer form
As if all emotion was gone
And yet she had to stay strong to get through
To be quiet so as to not awake, the ones who
Deserve to rest after a busy day
She wasn't tired anyway

As the clock strikes one
'Another day had begun'

She would fathom her woes
And ponder upon her misfortunes
And curse the cruelty of the lessons learned
As she remained still, a weak pawn
In someone else's game

She has no name
No ambition

For she cannot articulate nor understand who she
is
And what the world wants to see, has forever
clouded her mind
Made her forget her worth

For she fails to understand
How she must be, and so she pretends
To be someone she's not
Someone who fought
Her own shadow, a disfigured image
One she hoped she was not to be
Because a failure she cannot bear to see

She is a soul of few words
A heart of gold
But now afraid of love
For she's scared of a day that may come
When a friend goes cold
And a crack becomes a stab in her back
And before she knows it
Her light's gone black

Her conscious- a ghost
Her mind unstable
Her heart now broke
Tired, weak
She cannot talk
She begins to weep

She remembers then,
She only overthinks
'It cannot happen again'
Can it?
Though she has always been one to lend a
helping hand
She would give her heart to anyone who would
demand
It was too bad she had a soft spot for anyone
A stranger, an enemy or a friend

'Oh, but I must be careful'
She thought to herself
'Maybe playing some music would help?'
But her rhythms reflect
What her heart could not weigh
And her mind could not accept
Music was truly an art that wept

'Never mind' she thought
This will make me unhappy
'Maybe I should draw something
Or write in my diary'

But little did she know, that her book held
months
Of raw emotion of her early adolescence
About her struggling mother

With a daughter
Wishing she had sons

And the bullies in class
And the popular, smart kids
And her frizzy hair
And the homework she didn't finish

Flipping through the old pages
She couldn't bear
To realize that her worries
Had started then and there

She closed the book shut
She hears a step
No snoring, her father's awake
Her heart skips a beat
She rushes to her bed
And pretends to be asleep
Praying she doesn't lose a head

A few minutes pass by
Silence haunts her as she stays still
Finally she hears it
a slight snoring to her appeal
'Let me stay silent a little more.
Just to be sure'

But being tucked in a warm embrace
Of a blanket covered up to her face
Her eyelids fall heavy
Her muscles relax
She thinks to herself
'I am tired perhaps.'

And so off she drifts
In a moment or two
To a far away sleep
Where the skies aren't blue
And the clouds rained dew

A dreamy land
A peaceful scene
Everything feeling calm and serene
An escape from her reality
It was indeed

Betrayal's cruel lesson

Going to bed, with a heart in shatters,
weighing more than a sky held by Atlas
The heart breaking, once again
The brain's warnings were in vain

'You knew you would get hurt!'
'You knew what you were agreeing to!'
Yet never had I claimed my loyalty to be
A sign of my approval to entirely
Take advantage of me.

And yet no matter how much a good deed
I do, the ones who received it
This time, were deceiving me to
Believe that they were to be true
And honest companions

My eyes fill with the thought
That perhaps this time, t'was I who most lost my
dignity, my pride
My motivation and strife
And perhaps the only thing keeping me alive
My sugarcoated easy life

It hurts that I was used
most callously, unsparingly
Still, perhaps a hidden lesson
I've learned, unknowingly

The open-minded, kindhearted
Ones may give pity
But trusting people mustn't
be done light-heartedly

Hear ye, hear all
It's the end of the day
My final call, I want to say:
My scars will heal, My future arise
My enemies will soon meet their demise
And the ones who hate, shall soon meet their fate

For it is only those who learn and dream
From traumas, they will wipe off clean
A paradise, most pleasant waiting
For the ones who deserve, to get their happy
ending.

The betrayal that once broke a heart to shards
Has helped me mature, and taught something new
to my heart.

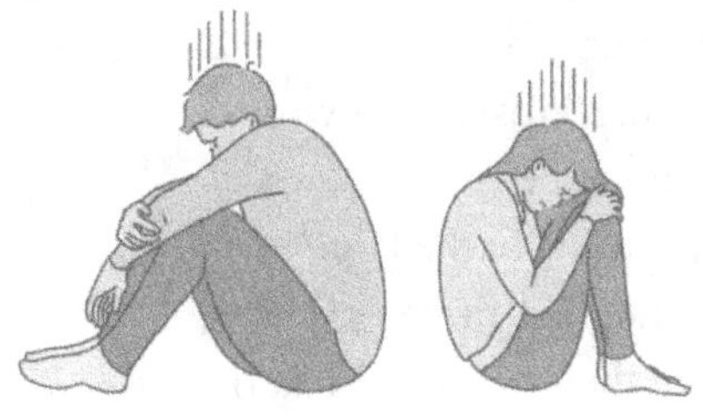

A Red hot flame

My fists in a ball and muscles tense
My heart beating rapid
My arms shaking with fury
My dark thoughts made valid
My goodness! How much this angers me
I've turned into a creature no one can tame
A burning red hot flame

All I see is a target
Someone to shoot at
With words made to pierce
I shouted and spat
A most triggering emotion
Made me spew all spite
I've become a burning hot flame
Red and bright

After moments had passed
Of heated hatred
Filled with a crossfire of words
Not meant to be said
I walked away, in the hope to end
The burning hot fire on my end
I realised then, what had I said
How very much I had been in my head

That hurtful moment of instant regret
Of the things said in anger
My heart filled with dread

The red hot flame after being expunged
I relaxed a bit and thought of what had happened
I couldn't believe what a monster I became
Blinded with hatred, vex, anger and pain
I tried to apologise for what I did
But since that day, our friendship ended.

Courage

Once a young boy seated in his place
Quiet and patient
Waiting for his teacher's announcement,
"You must all present your projects to the class."

A shiver of dread fell upon him
"No no no!
This cannot be happening!
I cannot bring myself to speak in front of them!
They will laugh and mock my presentation again!"

But what choice did he have?
He couldn't say no
He started with his work
For he had only three days more

Many a time he thought to give up
And tell his teacher he couldn't do it.
But what an embarrassment that would be
He would be teased for making such a plea

But remember what happened last time?
It hadn't gone well, he failed and cried
But this time, he was willing to try
To drive his shyness away and bring out his pride

He refused to let his hard work go to waste
He told himself, as he took his place
In the front of the class, all heads turned forward
All glaring, and staring in silence as he began

He took a deep breath, smiled and sighed his fears
away
He must display some courage today
And wow! I must say, he did so well!
If he was ever afraid, no one could tell!

In the end I'm happy to say
That young boy showed immense courage that day
I'm sure you too can overcome a fear
No matter your age,
If you have some courage
the things holding you back shall disappear.

Butterflies

I hope one day to fall in love
Like the couples in movies
Destined to be
Or like my favourite characters
from the many books I read
Or like the love-and-tease relationship my
parents have shown me.

I want to experience the foreign feeling
Of being struck by an arrow of Cupid
Of the blushing when you lock eyes
Of the 'butterflies in my stomach'
And the flutters in my heart,
Of the passionate emotions when you realise
That you want to be with them all of the time.

I've only heard of how magical
this phenomenon is
I've only seen from afar the lengths
People go to for the ones they love.
It seems impossible to me how someone can
Love another so much.

I can only wish upon the stars
That butterflies fly my way and

Share with me their magic
Of making minutes feel like hours
Of turning 'mine' to 'ours'
Of making strangers want to cherish each other
Of giving handwritten letters
And making them give and receive flowers
Of dancing together in the floral showers
Of their happy ending in each other's arms.

I hope one day to fall in love.

What keeps me up at night

It has always kept me up at night
Why do people hate and fight?
Why is our world so divided by religion, habits
And colour of the skin?
Is it the baby's fault that his mother
Is a darker shade than the others?
Is it the native's fault that they were born
Where the sun burns hot, and they require more
melanin than you?
Is it the girl's fault she was born with two Xs
And not one?
What has the little girl even done?
And yet they make her regret even being one.

It has always kept me up at night,
Why do people hate and fight?
And draw borders to separate and divide
Instead of celebrating our differences
Join together and unite?
Why wage wars for the use of guns?
Why not grow crops for the people
And spend time with your daughters and sons?
Why not share what you have
In return for something you need back?
Why so greedy for land?

Why not give the poor and starving their
demand?

Why bully someone for who they like?
Why can't you just let them live their life?
Why is it so hard for people to be kind?
How does our crippling mental health get turned
a blind eye?

It has always kept me up at night,
Why do some people still have no access to their
rights?
There still exists even today,
The starving, the thirsty, the poor, the abused
and the raped
How come we achieved to create an AI,
But can't even feed and quench the thirst of the
millions who die?
What's sad is that everyone knows
About them, but only a few show-up
To try and solve the problem.

I no longer see the world in black and white
But in shades of grey,
some dark and some light
Because I know everyone who has lived beyond
year five
Has done things both wrong and right.
I do not believe hell nor heaven exists

No gods, devils and angels, in the afterlife amidst
Because everyone has a new, and different perspective to give
For what they did and why
I believe you simply live your mortal life and die
Burnt, or buried, your body and consciousness are destroyed.
In fact I've realized, death is what gives value to life.

Things like these have always kept me up at night,
With the hope that one day, I will get to make some of these things right

When I Smile

Sometimes when I smile, I don't really mean it
I would rather be somewhere else
Or I'd rather cry, in fact
But I put on an act so well, no one would know
That my 'happiness' was not the truth,
But a show.

Sometimes when I laugh
I would much rather scream in anger
Because, they don't know what I know.
But I've learned to make it believable
I cover it up so well, they would never uncover
If it was the truth I showed.

Sometimes I want to smile
But with my mind in a trance
My lips refuse to lift themselves up
A force of some kind holds me back, making me
believe
'If things are this good, someone is going to
leave.
You cannot be this happy, something bad is
about to happen'

But sometimes, truly happy

And I laugh my heart out
I feel open and free
As if sorrow doesn't exist
Careless yet carefree

Times when my parents are pulling each other's
legs
Or, When I act silly with friends
Or even when I'm alone in my room, scrolling
through
Watching something amusing on YouTube

Times like these are when I laugh
And smile, hiding nothing inside
Putting all worries and overwhelming thoughts
aside
And pouring my joy-filled heart outside.
Not every laugh and smile
Of mine, was a lie…

The Cycle of Life

I watch the sea, as the water comes running in
I listen, to the rustling and crashes of waves
before they charge towards the sand.
After just seconds upon reaching for my feet
The water goes back from where it came
Further dampening the sand.
Another wave appears,
And continues the cycle as it has for years.

At times, even my emotions and thoughts
Swallow me in waves,
Each slightly stronger than the other
With each emotion my rationality caves
It feels like I'm drowning in my head
and I cannot swim out,
What's worse is that no one is around to see it,
And get me out

One after another, dark thoughts emerge
I try to scream, but my cries are muffled and
meek.
I try to cry, but another thought tells me-
"Crying is for the weak. You must not be seen as
weak!"

As my tear dries up, before it has even left my
eye.
Angry at myself for my vulnerability
I throw across the room, my pillows and clothes,
the only things next to me.
My heart prays simultaneously, for a day to be
free.

Free from what? You may ask?
Free from the judgemental eyes of society
Free from grades defining my worth
Free from being held in chains of self-hatred and
jealousy
Free from being guilty about not doing the
things I wish I could
Free from seeing others suffer, with no
capability to help them
Free from drowning in silence, because I have
no one I can trust
No one I can talk to, no one who would
understand.

Why cannot we live our lives in peace?
Still and calm like a lake,
Friendly and gentle like a cool breeze,
Like water, adaptable to change.
Not like a fire, destroying everything in its way.

Why must people judge how others live their
lives?
Destroying their self-esteem and pride.
Why not accept and celebrate them, like a new
sunrise?
Is it so hard to think of others? To say and do
something nice?
I cannot lose faith in humanity twice.

Why not accept the change in life?
Like the cycles of the day and night.
And the balance of dark and light
And black and white.
The balance and importance of dreams and
fears.
The cycle of life, as it has been for years.

Exam Time

The finals are coming
The preparations have begun
All chatter from students is about
How they want to score more this term.

Some say they'll do better
Some say they'll do worse
Some feel ready while some others are anxious.
And some are shocked at the amount of syllabus
and work.

Revision tests everyday
All study and work but no play.
I suppose for two months that should be okay.

All our heads in our books,
Highlighting paragraphs, memorising notes.
Relearning things we forgot
Things we ought to have not

Assignments, submissions
Essays, debates
Now, many wish they hadn't
Left those delayed
For the pressure now is immense

Not only from teachers and friends
But also our parents

Now it starts to hit you,
'I must study hard.
Or they'll think I'm no longer smart'
You can't let your social status suffer
If there were marks you couldn't cover.

You get on with work,
Day and night
Math, English, Social and Science.
You tell yourself-
"C'mon, brain! Just this once.
I need to get through the final exams!"
As you aggressively flip
through the damaged dog-eared pages
Of a language you don't understand.

On the first day of the finals, the atmosphere
intense,
In a few minutes the exam will commence!
You see everyone biting their nails and lips
Sweating, praying to the heavens
that the exam goes well.
You notice some have even given up hope
And have left it up to fate,
You suppose only time will tell
If you prepared enough for this date.

But within the blink
Of a turtle's eye (yes, a turtle)
The exams are over,
so quickly they went by
And you celebrate with friends,
as you walk out into the halls
Everyone is excited, already making plans for
the malls,
But you realise now… the stress taken
Was not needed at all
Everything went well, I hope, after all

And hey! Now it's time to enjoy the rest of your
days
You can finally rest, and put a smile on your
face…
Well, until the results come out,
It's a scare… always.

If I had money

What would I do if I had money?
Like uncountable money
Well, I can assure you
The outcome would be funny.

My first bill would be for chocolates and ice
cream,
I would make my room, the room of my dreams.
I would get myself, friends and family
Things they've always wanted, with my money.
And then I'd host a party,
With delicious food, and gallons of coffee
I am responsible too
So, I will make sure that I get only the best
Biodegradable packing and eco-friendly supplies

I would then wonder after a month
what to do with so much.
At this point I would invest, donate
and help others with my wealth
I am aware too that
Being wealthy comes with fake friends
So I would need to be careful
For with many my relation might end.

Later I would see,
If money can aid in pursuing my dreams
So successful I want to be
that I can go to sleep,
After having eaten some good ice cream.
In a bed, nice and fluffy
With a healthy happy family
And a calm, peaceful mind.

A heart of broken gold

I have always been,
A kind-hearted little thing,
Raised to share, and do good
A reared heart of gold.
The world seemed everything
but harmful and cold
But I've realized there's a problem
With my good-natured empathy
People exist in this world
Who seek to destroy you mentally
Who will take advantage of
Every ounce of what you give
And the worst part is,
I feel entitled to forgive,
Because 'everyone deserves a second chance'
Isn't it?

Being kind can be a curse,
Sometimes it makes things worse
I was just trying to be helpful,
But then they say- "what is your problem?"
And "mind your own business"
And all sorts of trouble.

Over and over,
I kept trusting
And cracking
until you stop caring anymore and
then they say- "you've changed"
"You were such a sweetheart"
"You had a golden heart."

And I say- It's broken now
Maybe it's the heart of broken gold

The lost smile

"Say cheese!", I follow instinctively
But of course, the smile comes out terribly

Somehow, I feel, I've lost the natural sparkle in
my eyes
My cheerful, innocent and natural smile
I'm not sure when it evaporated
For now it ceases to show
Now I find it horribly difficult
To radiate joy and glow

I practice in front of the mirror
My smile, with no one else near
But even after hours of trying
With crooked teeth and awkward smiling
The asymmetrical hair lining
The several angles I attempted denying
I walk out of the bathroom, nearly crying
My eyes fill with tears
Tears of guilt for ruining all pictures
Where I'm present
Tears of pain, that I cannot change it
Tears of self-hatred, that I have
grown to be like this

Is it so much to ask for,
To have a pretty natural smile?
And not a plastered mask on my face
A well-dressed lie?
I'm not sure why,
I cannot smile anymore
Even after trying a million times more

I hope one day
I can get back my smile…
And need no longer
Be wearing a lie.

Till then, I guess it's alright
Smile is not the only fight.

Who I want to be

It seems like everyone else knows
Exactly what they wish to be
But I'm clueless when I'm asked
Who I see, in the future of me

I search and search
And continue the journey
As fly through the options in my head
Author, dancer, singer, or a doctor
I lay awake at night in my bed.

How do I determine, what I should be?
How do I figure out my destiny?
What I'll be doing with my mind and body
For the rest of my life?

Days become weeks
And weeks become months
And still ongoing, for a career I hunt
While my creativity lies asleep.

"C'mon! Think!
What do you like doing?"
I beat myself up for not knowing
What role in life I want to be pursuing.
Why must a dream job be so hard in finding?

Soon I'll be taking the test,
And I'll need to choose!
And when that day comes
I can give no excuse.
Why is this so difficult?
I'm terribly confused!

But I suppose, whatever I choose
There are some things, some values
That I want to follow no matter what I do.

More than anything else,
I would want to be a kind human.

Kind, Happy and Free,
A person like that
is Who I want to be.

The Quite Kid

What does it mean to feel like an outcast,
when your happiness with big groups never last
because you don't really know what to say.
That feeling of being alone, even in a class of
twenty
Time ticking slowly, and you wanting to scream.

I would rather sit at the back, and never make a
sound,
Invisible almost.
They would ask why I don't talk much or come
ahead,
I would say- "I prefer to watch and listen
instead."
I would take pride in being the only one
with a book in hand
And immerse myself, in mystical lands.
Of stories like Harry Potter, or Peter Pan.
Or underrated ones, filled with unpredictable
irony,
blasphemy and romance.

And from there watch, as everyone
chattered in groups of their own
as if they were where they belong.

and laughed in the halls as they walked
while I stared longingly to have someone
with whom I could have a heart-to-heart talk.

Elders would tell me
To engage more, and befriend
But now I find it's not that easy
To give and extend
My hand in trust and friendship.
Because once upon a time,
I was social and confident
I grew up a bit, learned some hard lessons
And now I care what people think.
I don't know how to be
that confident little girl again.

Have you ever noticed around you
the silent ones, with their story
How the clouds roll up and
make the beautiful moon hid
One of those, I guess
I'm that quiet kid.

Sunshine in the cold

Hope is an enchanting thing
It's like finding a daffodil in a field of dry land
It's like finding an oasis after looking at miles of
sand
It's like finding long rays of sunshine
In your dark, dreary room
During the cold winter's gloom
It's like finding someone to help you up
When you're sinking fast in quicksand

It's like finding the North Star when you're lost
It's like finding ten bucks on the ground
When you couldn't bear the debts cost
It's like having a teddy to hug with when you are
having bad thoughts
It's like hearing motivating words when you are
going through a lot
It's finding a flashlight, the demons at night haunt
It's the only thing that keeps you going when all is
distraught
It's what helps you finally reach your goal
Have hope, it's the most enchanting thing.

Magical Moments

There are times
when you want the time to stop
There are moments
you wish, are not momentary
When there is a radiant glow on your face
charged by the sparks of happiness
as if every cell of the body
is celebrating a common party

These are the pitstops
which keep us going
which makes us forget all worries
and takes us to our infancy
It's an emotion so pure,
Only a mother holding her child for the first
time, can endure

This can be found in the smallest of things like a
dew drop
and silliest of jokes, which no one else
understands
and it can even come when doing the toughest
task

when we enjoy the process, and not worry about
the result!
It can come with an old picture triggering a
memory
and it can come with a hard-fought success

Everyone knows how critical these are
Yet no one can manufacture it
To create them, there can be no magic and no
ploy
Such moments my friend, are the moments, of
true joy

My Happy Place

After a long tiring day,
Seeing a simple 'good night' text,
from a friend, can make my day.

After having an argument with someone close
Coming back to my room
Behind my closed doors
My music helps me heal
It becomes my safe space.

After crying my eyes out
From not liking how I look
A comment and a hug from my best friends
Telling me how much they love me
Can lighten up my mood

On days when I feel worthless
And unappreciated
My parents telling me they are proud
Means so much to me

When someone remembers details
Of me when we talked last
Can make me so happy
Knowing that they cared enough to listen to me

It's the little things that people do
That make me the happiest
A simple gesture, a greeting
A compliment or a hug
Can lift my whole day up

In my room, with music and headphones on, or,
being part of my parents pulling pranks on each
other, or,
having long walks with friends and talking
endlessly
or sometimes just nothing and yet understanding

That, for me, is my happy place.

The success of success

Ah! The rush of pride in my chest
When I finally accomplish something
Is something I crave when
I try to take on a challenge
Or when I'm asked to do some
Out of my comfort zone

I've been told often
that I keep my expectations high
But a wise someone once said
"Your dreams are not big enough
if they don't scare the hell out of you"
Trying is great, because you learn something new!

Maybe it does bum me down
When I cannot reach what I set out for
But after all, I tried my best
Meaning in the end
It was still a success!

To be a friend

Well you could be a genuine acquaintance
Or a person I rarely pass by
A person I could have small talk with
Just a "hello!" And "bye!"
Or you could be a person I talk to everyday
Someone I can tell, the gossip of the day
Someone I would invite to go to a party
Or you could be an old family friend
Like a brother or sister I shared a mother with
Or you are someone I'm very close to
Someone I can come to
When I feel down
Or you could be someone I talk to online
Or you could be someone I would call
To have fun with, and go party
Or someone I could text any time
And they would immediately reply.

But only my best friend,
Can be all this in one.

In the heart of a teenager

This stage in life
Is a difficult one
So much so that scientists study
To learn more about us
And what goes on in our heads
When we make certain decisions

We are part-child and part-adult
We learn and grow faster
We change, and emotions are enhanced
We do things adults don't understand

Changes affect us to the core
Things that happen to us at this age
Remain with us forever
As our minds are still growing and fragile

We find it frustrating when
Parents and teachers do not comprehend
Our outbursts and breakdowns
And emotions of anger and pain

We go through stress,
And pressure
And crushes, and breakups

And losing friends
And making amends
And trying everything to 'fit in'
It's a complicated stage of
everything you can think of

We are told often
That we are too young to know
What is right and wrong
We are scolded when we question
The 'why' of how things are
We are either "too old"
Or "too young".

All we wish is to be understood
And to be asked about our perspectives
About life as we know it
From the heart of a teenager.